WHEN
BAD THINGS
HAPPEN TO
GOOD MARRIAGES

WORKBOOK FOR HUSBANDS

HOW TO STAY TOGETHER
WHEN LIFE PULLS YOU APART

WHEN BAD THINGS HAPPEN TO GOOD MARRIAGES

WORKBOOK FOR HUSBANDS

Drs. Les & Leslie Parrott

ZONDERVAN™

GRAND RAPIDS, MICHIGAN 49530

ZONDERVAN™

When Bad Things Happen to Good Marriages Workbook for Husbands
Copyright © 2001 by Les and Leslie Parrott

Requests for information should be addressed to:
Zondervan, *Grand Rapids, Michigan 49530*

ISBN: 0-310-23902-8

Interior design by Rob Monacelli

Printed in the United States of America

04 05 06 07 / ❖ CH / 10 9 8 7 6 5 4

Contents

A Letter to Our Readers

I took a speed reading course and read *War and Peace* in twenty minutes," says comedian Woody Allen. "It involves Russia."

Ever felt like that after reading a book? Sometimes it becomes so easy to focus on finishing a book that we miss its main message. What you hold in your hand is a kind of insurance policy against that happening while you are reading *When Bad Things Happen to Good Marriages*. But it's more than that, too.

Books let us shake hands with new ideas. But these ideas remain as flat as the printed page if we do not apply them to our lives. For this reason, we have designed workbooks—one for husbands and one for wives—that will help you incorporate into your marriage the new lessons you learn while reading.

As you read through the main book, you will discover places where it points you to do an exercise in these workbooks. Most of them are designed for you to take about five minutes on your own to complete a few questions or to take a brief self-test and then compare your results with your spouse (that's why it's important for each spouse to have a workbook). Or, it may give you an exercise to do together so that you can put into practice a new principle. This is where real learning occurs. This is where new ideas become more than acquaintances; they begin to make a positive difference in your marriage.

We have used these exercises with countless couples, both in our counseling practice as well as in our seminar settings. They are proven. They work. And that's why we are passionate about you doing them as you read through our book.

While there is no one right way to use these workbooks, we suggest that you complete the exercises as you encounter them in the book, or soon after you have finished reading the chapter that covers the exercise. In other words, try to complete the exercises for that chapter before moving on to the next one. The point is to integrate the exercises into the process of reading the book. Some of the exercises are designed to be used again and again ("The Big Question," for example), helping you continue to deepen your level of intimacy. Others are more of a one-shot exercise designed to give you a flash of insight.

As you proceed through the pages of this book, make it your own. Don't get too hung up on following the rules. If a particular exercise leads you down a more intriguing path, take it. Some of these exercises may simply serve as springboards to discussions that fit your style more appropriately. However, if an exercise seems a bit challenging, don't give up on it. As the saying goes, anything worth having is worth working for—especially when it comes to marriage.

So, whether you are a speed reader or not, we hope you don't approach *When Bad Things Happen to Good Marriages* just to check it off your "to-do" list. We hope and pray that you will, instead, use these exercises, self-tests, and discussion questions to internalize the book's message and fortify your marriage with every possible good thing.

LES AND LESLIE PARROTT

Exercise 1:

TAKING INVENTORY OF THE GOOD AND THE BAD

Every couple bumps into bad things—circumstances that make marriage more difficult. In this first exercise, we urge you to take an inventory of "bad things" threatening your love. Every couple has their own unique list. What follows are some of the most common. Take a moment, without input from your spouse, to check those that currently top your list.

_____ Frequent conflict

_____ Financial pressures

_____ Power struggles

_____ Busy schedules

_____ Work pressures

_____ Career crisis

_____ Infertility

_____ Tumultuous relations with extended family

_____ A rebellious child

_____ Sexual unfulfillment

_____ Lack of spiritual intimacy

_____ Frequent communication breakdowns

_____ Major illness

_____ Addictions

_____ Infidelities and lack of trust

_____ Grief or loss

_____ Other: __________________________

Before discussing the list you just made with your partner, take a few more minutes to note the things in your life right now that are good for your marriage. What half dozen good things are augmenting the love you share? Your list could consist of anything from "having a date night each week" to "being honest with each other" to "sharing the housework." Note what is currently going on that buoys your marriage in spite of bad things.

_____ Being honest with each other

_____ Sharing housework

_____ Sharing humor or laughter

_____ Having strong social support

_____ Sharing a vision for our future

_____ Enjoying a committed church life together

_____ Enjoying a fulfilling sex life

_____ Having a date night

_____ Enjoying good children

_____ Feeling in good physical health

_____ Having a secure financial future

_____ Sharing interests and hobbies

_____ Enjoying strong extended family relationships

_____ Supporting each other in prayer

_____ Feeling secure in our marriage commitment

_____ Feeling strong emotional health

_____ Other: _______________________________

Once you've made your two lists, set aside some time to share this information with each other. Don't turn this into a gripe session. The point of sharing your first list is to simply identify what difficult things you are both contending with that impact your marriage. The goal in sharing your second list is to remember the good, not just the bad.

Exercise 2:

How "Good" Is Your Marriage?

This brief exercise requires honesty, sensitivity, and self-reflection. As you read in the book, research has revealed five qualities that are the armament used to protect good couples from the destruction of bad things:

- Ownership — taking responsibility for what you do and say
- Hope — believing that good is a part of your future
- Empathy — putting yourself in your partner's shoes
- Forgiveness — letting go of resentment and making things right
- Commitment — doing all you can to make your relationship rock solid

As you consider these qualities, rate where you, and then your partner, are on each one. Do this on your own, without consulting your mate for now.

You as a Husband

Shift Blame	1	2	3	4	5	Take Ownership
Pessimistic	1	2	3	4	5	Optimistic
Self-Consumed	1	2	3	4	5	Empathic
Resentful	1	2	3	4	5	Forgiving
Give Up Easily	1	2	3	4	5	Fully Committed

Your Wife

Shift Blame	1	2	3	4	5	Take Ownership
Pessimistic	1	2	3	4	5	Optimistic
Self-Consumed	1	2	3	4	5	Empathic
Resentful	1	2	3	4	5	Forgiving
Give Up Easily	1	2	3	4	5	Fully Committed

After both you and your partner have rated these qualities on your own, take a few minutes to discuss your results. It is important to stay objective in this discussion. Focus on being sensitive to your partner's feelings and being open to what your partner has to say. The goal is to learn what both of you bring to your joint efforts in battling bad things.

Exercise 3:

WHY GOOD MARRIAGES BUMP INTO BAD THINGS

The more you understand *why* bad things happen to good marriages, the better equipped you are to transcend the bad things. Knowing *why* empowers our *how*. So this simple exercise is devoted to helping you, on your own without your partner's input for now, identify which causal factors are most likely to sabotage your relationship. Begin by reflecting for a moment on some of the difficulties your marriage has faced. If you were to sum up your explanation for *why* these things have happened, how would you put it?

____

____

____

____

Next, review the list of explanations given in the book and rank them from 1 (the most accurate reason that applies to your marriage) to 5 (the least accurate reason your marriage has bumped into bad things).

The main reason for our marriage experiencing difficulty right now is . . .

_____ My Idealistic Expectations

_____ My Restless Sense of Self

_____ My Lack of Relationship Skills

_____ My Unhealthy Choices

_____ Our Unfortunate Circumstances

Once you have given each of these potential reasons a ranking, share them with your partner and compare your answers as you discuss why your good marriage is most vulnerable to bad things.

12

Exercise 4:

What Did You Expect?

Most unrealistic expectations we have about our marriage are fueled by thoughts and feelings we are not even aware of. For example, we may have an expectation about how our partner is to care for the yard or prepare a meal—something we've never really articulated to ourselves or anyone else—but only when our partner doesn't fulfill our expectation do we become aware of how important our expectation is. As you look back over your married life, what unrealistic expectations can you identify?

____

____

____

____

To help you identify more specific expectations that are not getting met in your marriage, consider the following list of common expectations and note which ones you used to have and which ones you still are holding on to today:

	In the Past	Still Expecting	New Expectation
My spouse should . . .			
Always listen attentively	______	______	______
Stay at home with the kids	______	______	______
Work full-time	______	______	______
Manage the family finances	______	______	______
Do the yard work	______	______	______
Care for our automobile(s)	______	______	______
Prepare a hot meal each evening	______	______	______
Schedule social events	______	______	______
Do the grocery shopping	______	______	______

	In the Past	Still Expecting	New Expectation
Surprise me with gifts on occasion	_____	_____	_____
Plan our vacations	_____	_____	_____
Initiate sex	_____	_____	_____
Keep the house clean	_____	_____	_____
Want to discuss our relationship	_____	_____	_____
Know what I'm thinking	_____	_____	_____
Go to bed when I do	_____	_____	_____
Consult me on decisions	_____	_____	_____
Discipline our children	_____	_____	_____
Plan our date nights	_____	_____	_____
Other: _______________	_____	_____	_____

Once you have noted your expectations, both from the past and the present, share your lists with each other and keep in mind that this is simply an exercise in sharing information. We will get to solutions to unrealistic expectations shortly.

THE BIG QUESTION

You've read about how we all have blind spots that only our spouse can help us see. This exercise will facilitate a healthy exchange between the two of you so that you can discuss these with a minimum of defensiveness. This is an exercise, by the way, that you can do on a weekly or monthly basis. It takes no more than ten minutes, and here's how it works.

1. Ask your partner if she is willing, along with you, to answer "The Big Question": What would make me a better spouse?

2. If she agrees, prepare your mind to be objective and open to giving as well as receiving personal information. Lower your guard and warm your heart.

3. On scratch paper, note one thing your wife could do right now to be a better marriage partner to you.

4. On that same paper, note one thing that already makes your wife a good marriage partner to you right now. Be sure you have in mind an example from the past week that backs up your point and makes it concrete.

5. Once you have both made your notes of one good thing and one area for improvement, take turns sharing what you have.

6. Finally, don't nag your wife about how she could improve—make your suggestion during this exercise and then leave it there, until the next time you do The Big Question.

So Many Choices

Geoffrey Fisher, archbishop of Canterbury, once noted that every man and woman makes personal choices in the "sacred realm of privacy." At the risk of being too bold, we ask you, in this exercise, to allow your spouse into this sacred realm and explore the choices you both have made—choices that have served as a rudder to your marriage. These are choices that have brought your marriage to the place it is today. The book notes several examples of negative kinds of choices (keeping information private, withholding sex, going into debt, breaking a confidence with your spouse, not seeking counseling when you needed it, etc.). Take a moment right now to note a half dozen personal choices that are relevant; three choices for the better and three for the worse.

Three choices I/we made that improved our marriage:

1. ____

2. ____

3. ____

Three choices I/we made that worsened our marriage:

1. ____

2. ____

3. ____

As you review these choices, what can you learn to improve your decision making as it relates to your relationship?

____

____

____

____

Exercise 7:

COPING WITH THE INVASION OF INTIMACY

Not every spouse sees this issue as a significant one. So before going much further, rate how intimacy has become an invasion for you in your marriage on the following scale.

Not a problem   Major problem

1   2   3   4   5   6   7   8   9   10

Now rate on this same scale how you think your spouse might answer. Next, compare how your partner answered with how you thought she would.

If either you or your spouse rated this issue at a five or higher, continue on with this exercise to more effectively put into practice coping strategies for your situation.

The book suggests that you make known to your partner what is off limits for you because it is too vulnerable, too painful. In specific terms, what topics of conversation, what incidents, what secrets do you need to underscore with your spouse? Briefly note these tender spots and explain to your partner why these things are off limits.

____

____

____

____

The book also suggests that you create personal space by drawing some boundary lines. For example, if you need time to decompress at the end of the day before you jump into a conversation or before you get hit with a list of errands or things you need to do, make your needs explicitly known. Maybe you need an evening a month with your buddies to maintain that connection. Whatever it is, in the space below note specific things that would help you gain the space you need to become more fully present with your partner, and then share it with her.

____

____

____

____

____

The book suggests one more thing that will help you cope with an overabundance of intimacy: Draw a property line. What personal items do you want left alone? Perhaps it is your newspaper, a special pen you keep on your desk, or any number of things that you are especially wanting to be sure are left the way you want them. Make these known in the space below and share them with your partner.

____

____

____

____

____

Exercise 8:

WHEN HUSBAND AND WIFE BECOME MOM AND DAD

As the book points out, a new mom and a new dad each have their own role in keeping a good marriage going. Dads need to work at entering their wives' new world, and moms need to give their husbands space to do so. For this reason, the exercises for this section in your two workbooks are quite different but will take you toward the same goal.

Especially for dads: As you read in the book, the majority of wives experience a huge plummet in their marital satisfaction in the year after their first baby arrives. Your dissatisfaction usually kicks in later—in reaction to your wife's unhappiness. If you want to alleviate much of the inevitable marital dissatisfaction for both of you, you've got to expand your sense of "one-ness" to a "we-ness" that includes your children. How do you do this? Only you can answer this question for sure, but it will probably mean being in touch with the changes that are taking place within you and talking about them with your wife. To begin with, rate your personal confidence level in being a good father.

Unsure of myself   Very confident in my role

1 2 3 4 5 6 7 8 9 10

As you try to embrace your new role as a father, you must give up trying to hold on to your pre-kid era. In specific terms, what things will you have to give up to be a good dad?

1. ____

2. ____

3. ____

Next, note ways you can tangibly embrace being a father and ways you can join your wife in this alteration of your marriage.

1. ____

2. ____

3. ____

It's up to you how much you want to share this information with your wife. Maybe you want to keep it to yourself for now as you work on these areas of personal growth. Or maybe you want to share your list with her to give you some sense of accountability. It's your call.

Exercise 9:

REFUELING THE SEXUAL FIRE

Talking about sex with your partner can be an intimidating experience. You may have had previous discussions in this area that only made matters worse. In this exercise, we want to guide you in a healthy, productive discussion with one primary goal: to understand each other's sexuality better. So set aside preconceived notions and focus on understanding—first, yourself, and then your spouse's sexuality.

Begin by rating your sexual desire in general on the following scale:

Weak sexual desire   Strong sexual desire

1   2   3   4   5   6   7   8   9   10

Next, consider how many times in a month you would ideally like to have sex with your spouse.

- Less than once a month
- Once a month
- Twice a month
- Once a week
- Twice a week or more

How do you know when your partner would like to have sex? What signs do you watch for?

____

____

____

____

____

How do you like sex to be initiated in your relationship? Is this something you like to do, or do you prefer your partner do this, and if so, how?

____

____

____

____

In your opinion, what is the major roadblock to enjoying sex with your partner? Is it busy schedules, lack of desire, hygiene, interruptions, shortage of romance? Identify what makes it difficult for you, personally, to enjoy a fulfilling sex life. If you do not have anything that is an impediment from your perspective, identify what you think your spouse might say.

____

____

____

____

Once you have completed these questions, take time to discuss your answers with each other. Are your levels of sexual desire quite different? If so, are you able to understand and make adjustments to your partner's level of desire? To do this, begin by identifying times when the two of you are most in synch sexually.

We are most sexually in synch when (we have had a date night, we have prayed together, we are away from the kids, we have both had a shower, etc.) . . .

____

____

____

____

Keep in mind that the goal of your conversation is simply to understand your partner's sexuality and think constructively about how you can create a more fulfilling sex life together. With this in mind, we urge you to brainstorm more things you can do as a couple to improve your sex life.

Exercise 10:

YOUR ATTITUDE QUOTIENT

You are engaging in self-talk every minute of your waking life. You use this internal thought language to interpret the world. And it is your self-talk that forms the basis for your attitude. This quick exercise will help you assess your attitude. Simply rate how much you agree with each of these statements by using the following scale.

1 Strongly disagree
2 Disagree
3 Not sure
4 Agree
5 Strongly agree

_____ I believe the maxim that says, "A zebra cannot change his stripes."

_____ If there is something wrong, I'll notice it.

_____ It is almost impossible to overcome the influences of the past.

_____ Sometimes the littlest thing can ruin my day.

_____ I tend to be more grumpy when the weather's bad.

_____ Some difficulties cannot be made better.

_____ If something doesn't work, I tend to give up.

_____ Nothing in life is free.

_____ I rarely get my share of the pie.

_____ There's always someone to blame.

_____ *Total "NT" Score*

Once you have added up your ratings for this list—what we call your "NT" score—proceed to the next list of statements and do the same thing.

_____ If a person wants to, he can be happy under almost any circumstances.

_____ I like the respect of others, but if I don't get it I'm not going to stew about it.

_____ People are disturbed not by situations but by the view they take of them.

_____ I cause my own moods.

_____ I believe that something good is around the corner.

_____ Just because something once affected your life doesn't mean it needs to still do so.

_____ People are basically trustworthy.

_____ I'm optimistic about the future.

_____ I'm good at adjusting to things beyond my control.

_____ People describe me as having a thick skin.

_____ *Total "PT" Score*

Add up your ratings for this list. It is your "PT" score.

Your NT score indicates the degree of negative thinking you tend to engage in. Your PT score indicates the degree of positive thinking you tend to do. By comparing these numbers, you can begin to determine whether you do more positive thinking than negative, or the other way around. If you both feel comfortable doing so, compare your scores with your spouse's scores.

Exercise 11:

WHAT HAVE YOU BEEN LOOKING FOR?

Everyone is looking for something—especially in marriage. We call it your mind-set, and understanding your marriage mind-set is one of the most important exercises a spouse can do. Your mind-set, after all, has nothing to do with anyone but you. This exercise will help you become aware of what you are looking for in your spouse and whether it is helpful to your marriage.

We all view our partner through a series of filters. Below is a list of these filters. Look through this list of filters and check the six or so that are most descriptive of the ways you view your partner.

____ Accepting	____ Gentle	____ Petty
____ Adaptable	____ Giving	____ Playful
____ Aggressive	____ Greedy	____ Principled
____ Annoying	____ Gruff	____ Protective
____ Anxious	____ Gullible	____ Rational
____ Bitter	____ Helpful	____ Reactionary
____ Brave	____ Helpless	____ Reasonable
____ Calm	____ Idealistic	____ Reassuring
____ Carefree	____ Inconsiderate	____ Regretful
____ Careless	____ Innovative	____ Relaxed
____ Caring	____ Insensitive	____ Reliable
____ Cheerful	____ Intelligent	____ Respectful
____ Clever	____ Irresponsible	____ Rigid
____ Cold	____ Irritable	____ Self-conscious
____ Confident	____ Jealous	____ Self-righteous
____ Conforming	____ Kind	____ Spontaneous
____ Controlling	____ Lazy	____ Stubborn
____ Critical	____ Manipulative	____ Tactful
____ Demanding	____ Naïve	____ Tender
____ Dependable	____ Narcissistic	____ Trusting
____ Dependent	____ Negative	____ Trustworthy
____ Determined	____ Noisy	____ Understanding
____ Disciplined	____ Objective	____ Unpredictable
____ Efficient	____ Oblivious	____ Visionary
____ Elusive	____ Passive	____ Witty
____ Energetic	____ Patient	____ Worried
____ Friendly	____ Perfectionist	

Once you have checked the top half dozen ways you tend to view your spouse, determine whether they are mostly positive or mostly negative. The list is composed of forty filters in each category. In the space below, note the negative filters you tend to view your spouse through and when you are most likely to use them.

Filter: _____________. I see this quality when my spouse . . .
____.

Filter: _____________. I see this quality when my spouse . . .
____.

Filter: _____________. I see this quality when my spouse . . .
____.

Filter: _____________. I see this quality when my spouse . . .
____.

Filter: _____________. I see this quality when my spouse . . .
____.

Filter: _____________. I see this quality when my spouse . . .
____.

Next, consider ways that you might counter your negative filters with a more positive mind-set. You might ask your partner for ways that you could view a situation or a specific behavior more positively. You may want to consider the four steps outlined in chapter 4 and see how they might apply to your potentially negative mind-set. With an open mind, this discussion can be a turning point in changing your mind-set, not to mention your marriage, for the better.

Exercise 12:

TAKING CONTROL OF YOUR TIME-STARVED MARRIAGE

Since you are motivated to read our book and do these workbook exercises, we know that your marriage is a high priority for you. In this exercise, however, we want you to get more clear than you have ever been about this priority. More important, we want what you *say* about your marriage being important to match what you *do* about it.

You can begin to gain control of your time-starved marriage by taking a moment to answer a few basic questions.

How much time do you spend together in a typical workday? _______________________

How much time do you spend together in a typical weekend? _______________________

Total number of hours you spend together in an average week _______________

How do you spend the waking hours you have together each week? List as many specific activities as you can recall from a typical week.

____

____

____

____

____

Review the list you just made and circle the three most important activities you do together. Would you like more time to do these? If so, identify specific things you can do to create more time for them (e.g., eliminate another activity, start a baby-sitting co-op, schedule it in our calendars). The more specific you are, the better.

____

____

____

____

____

What things were not on your list but you wish they were? In other words, what do you wish you did together as a couple, but never seem to find the time for?

____

____

____

____

____

The key for most busy couples is making time for those activities which are not urgent but are important. The things you would like to have more time for get swallowed by urgent things that sometimes matter and sometimes don't. If you want to have a date night once a week, for example, you will need to protect that time ferociously. Take time right now to discuss with your spouse ways you will make your non-urgent, but important activities in your marriage a top priority by giving them the time they deserve.

Exercise 13:

GETTING TO KNOW YOU . . . ALL OVER AGAIN

This is an exercise designed to help you set the wheels in motion for reconnecting with your spouse. We begin with a brief assessment of simple questions:

Y   N   Has your sexual interest in each other waned in the last few months or years?

Y   N   Do you find yourself looking for alternatives to being with your spouse?

Y   N   Has celebrating her birthday become just another thing on your "to do" list?

Y   N   Do you depend less and less on your partner for information and activity?

Y   N   Do you deliberately plan events apart from your spouse?

Y   N   Have you quit sharing the details of your life with your spouse?

Y   N   If you have a choice, would you prefer to be with friends rather than your spouse?

The more you answered "Yes" to these questions, the wider the gap between you and your spouse. The question, of course, is how to bring the two of you closer together. And the key is getting reacquainted. Literally. Consider the following questions regarding your spouse:

1. What is her favorite recent movie?
2. What has she learned about herself in the past year?
3. What worries her the most right now?
4. What has she recently been thinking about her parents?
5. What is she most proud of doing in the last month?
6. What does she like most about you right now?
7. What is her favorite childhood memory?
8. What has touched her most deeply in recent days?
9. What is the best part of her day?

Can you answer these questions? This is just a start, but these kinds of questions will help you get to know your partner and bring you closer together. Take some time to explore these and other issues with her.

There are a couple more things we suggest in this exercise. Identify for yourself what is taking precedence over your marriage. Is your work, your activities at church, your children, your addiction, your painful past, or anything else crowding you out of time with your spouse? Take a serious look at your life right now, and if you see that something is keeping you from your marriage, write it down. Labeling it is the first step in changing it. So write it down and take a stab at identifying how you can keep it from further crowding out your marriage.

____

____

____

____

Next, make note of a specific plan to get away for a weekend together. In the space below, write down where, when, and how you might get away together within the next four weeks. Then look over the list of questions from the beginning of this exercise and add to it. What can you ask your spouse in order to get reacquainted with her? Make your list of questions here:

____

____

____

____

As the two of you steal away for your weekend together, make getting to know her your top goal. Explore the list of questions together, and reconnect with parts of your partner you have too long neglected.

Exercise 14:

HEALING YOUR PAINFUL PAST

This is not an exercise for everyone. Because we all have unique, personal stories, some will find this more helpful than others. It is designed to be a tool for talking to your partner about the pain from your past as a way to begin its healing.

Reflect on your personal history and make note of any memories you have of feeling hurt. The point here is not to dredge up minor offenses you have suffered, but rather more significant betrayals or injustices you have endured. No need to record all the details, just make a note of what it is that comes to mind.

____

____

____

____

____

As you explore these painful memories in your own mind, consider how they may have or are still impacting the way you relate to your spouse. This is your "unfinished business." If you feel safe enough, invite your spouse into this process by asking her to hear your story. Then, see if she has any ideas or theories about how your painful past continues to impact your present marriage. If you would like, you can record the insights you both might have in the following space.

____

____

____

____

____

As we note in the book, we urge you to seek help from a professional counselor if you believe previous pain is causing you marital difficulties. There are simply too many personal variables for you to make much long-term progress from a brief exercise. And be assured that there is hope for overcoming your painful past. In time, you will discover that this healing process has given you an unspeakable depth of connection to your partner and brought you to a marriage you've only dreamed about.

TAKING COVER FROM A BOMBSHELL AND ITS FALLOUT

The goal of this exercise is to help you ease into chapter 6 by giving you and your partner an opportunity to explore whatever crisis has struck your relationship. Take some time to explore the following issues, and you will be better equipped to move forward to some of the specific issues in this chapter.

To begin with, consider what you expected from married life. An earlier exercise in this workbook helped you explore some potentially unrealistic expectations most of us carry into this relationship, but what we are asking about here is your big picture. Talk to your partner about that picture. Did you ever imagine facing a crisis together? If so, what did you envision?

____

____

____

____

____

Next, explore how your particular marriage crisis shook you personally. Describe in specific terms how it has impacted you.

____

____

____

____

____

____

Complete the following sentences to help you clarify the impact of your crisis.

Before our marriage crisis . . . ___________________________

____

After our marriage crisis . . . ___________________________

____

The worst thing for my spouse involving our crisis . . . _______

____

The best thing for my spouse involving our crisis . . . ________

____

The worst thing for me to come out of our crisis . . . ________

____

The best thing for me to come out of our crisis . . . _________

____

If you feel safe enough, share with each other what you have gained from completing this exercise.

Exercise 16:

SURVIVING YOUR PRIVATE GETHSEMANE

Every couple who is jolted by a personal crisis—a private Gethsemane—is left wondering what to do to survive it. In this exercise we give you some concrete steps to consider.

First, acknowledge the loss. Things are not the same since your jolt. What have you lost? Make a list of everything that comes to mind, not just the obvious. For example, if your spouse has become a gambling addict, you have not only lost money because of the addiction, you have lost the spontaneity to go places where she may be especially tempted to gamble. You have lost the freedom to watch certain television programs because of it, and so on. Make a list of your losses.

____

____

____

____

Being aware of what you have lost is crucial to recovery. It will help you transcend denial and become more clearheaded and healthy. Next, assess where you are on your road to coming back from this jolt. Be honest and use the following scale if it is helpful.

In hopeless despair   Hopeful and moving on

1   2   3   4   5   6   7   8   9   10

If you are rating your situation as more hopeless than hopeful, what can you do, in specific terms (e.g., start a support group), that you are not already doing to make your recovery from this jolt more complete?

____

____

____

____

How will your marriage be stronger as a result of battling this crisis and overcoming this jolt?

———————————————————————————————

———————————————————————————————

———————————————————————————————

———————————————————————————————

———————————————————————————————

———————————————————————————————

If you feel safe enough, discuss this exercise with your partner.

Exercise 17:

OWNING UP

Taking responsibility for the state of your marriage can be one of the most challenging and humiliating actions a husband or wife ever faces. It is far easier to point fingers and lay blame than it is to stand up and say, "The buck stops here." This exercise, however, is designed to help you do just that.

How would you rate the current state of your marriage?

Lousy   Outstanding

1   2   3   4   5   6   7   8   9   10

How do you think your partner would rate the current state of your marriage?

Lousy   Outstanding

1   2   3   4   5   6   7   8   9   10

How much are you responsible for its current condition?

No responsibility   Complete responsibility

1   2   3   4   5   6   7   8   9   10

How much responsibility do you think your partner would take for the current state of your marriage?

No responsibility   Complete responsibility

1   2   3   4   5   6   7   8   9   10

At this point, if you feel safe enough, share and discuss the results of this part of the exercise with each other. Compare your answers and explain to each other why you answered the way you did.

Next, do your best to set aside your impulse to shift blame for anything that is not the way you want it in your marriage and identify in specific terms what you (though it may not be you alone) are responsible for. Don't get caught up in why you are not solely responsible; let that go for now and simply identify what you bring to the current state of your marriage.

I am responsible for . . . ________________________________

I am responsible for . . . ________________________________

I am responsible for . . . ________________________________

Share these things with your partner. As you listen to your spouse talk about what she is responsible for, do not compound her guilt. Simply listen carefully and be sure that she knows you are listening with a compassionate ear. You may want to take this exercise a step further—now or later—and identify what you will do about the things you know you are responsible for. You can use this space to identify one thing you will start or stop doing because you are responsible.

____

____

____

____

By the way, this is where accountability really pays off. Consider the idea of talking to a trusted friend who will keep your feet to the fire, a friend who will ask you routinely how you are doing at changing the behavior you have targeted.

Exercise 18:

HIGH HOPES — EVEN WHEN YOU'RE HURTING

Once you have established a reasonable level of responsibility, hope begins to bloom. You can't expect it to be soaring, but in time it will grow. For now, it is important to honestly determine how much you have. If your marriage ran on a tank of hope, where would the needle that measures its level be? Are you recently refueled, or are you running on fumes? Draw in the needle on this "hope gauge."

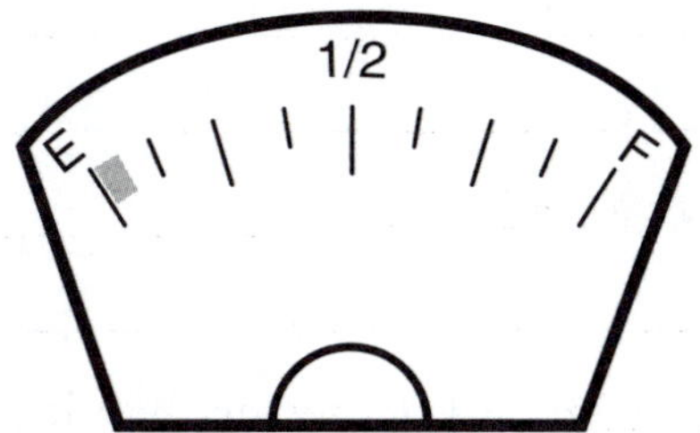

Many experts believe that optimism and hope are contagious. If your hope is sagging, consider someone, perhaps another couple you know, who has high hopes. Study them. What is it about their personality, their character, that cultivates hope? And if you think it's just "luck," think again. Optimistic people aren't lucky at all. They have disciplined themselves to see the light at the end of the tunnel when others think there is no end to their troubles in sight. Once you have identified a good model of hope, list two or three qualities that you think contribute to their optimism.

1. ____

2. ____

3. ____

What can you learn from them? Would you ever consider asking this person or this couple to be your hope mentors? Remember that if your marriage is to successfully battle bad things, you will need an ample supply of hope. So you must do all you can to cultivate it—even be mentored in it.

The bottom line is that hope has to do with the picture you have of your future. Take a moment right now to carefully envision the future of your marriage. What does it look like a year from now? Paint your picture with as many details as possible by completing these sentences:

The thing that worries me most about our future is . . . ______

____

____

The thing that gives me the most hope for the future of our marriage is . . . _____________________________________

____

A year from now, we will . . . _________________________________

____

In time, our marriage will be better than it is today because . . .

____

____

Share your answers with one another and discuss your future together by identifying the dreams and hopes you hold about it.

Exercise 19:

WALKING IN YOUR PARTNER'S SHOES

In the book, we point out that to really practice empathy, you must use both your heart and your head. In other words, empathy requires both a feeling and a thinking component. Like two wings of an airplane, empathy needs your capacity to sympathize as well as analyze. And if you are like most people, you are probably better at loving more with either your head or your heart. Take this quick test to uncover your love style.

1. When my wife brings home a problem, I usually try to . . .
   a. solve it so she is less troubled.
   b. simply let her know I understand.

2. If my wife has a cold or allergy and needs something from the pharmacy, I typically . . .
   a. try to get it when I am out on other errands.
   b. drop everything else to get it as soon as possible.

3. When my wife is experiencing deep emotions, I try to . . .
   a. help her get them under control.
   b. feel the same feelings with her.

4. Which describes you better?
   a. I tend to be objective
   b. I tend to be sympathetic

The more times you answered with "a," the more likely you are to love with your head. The more times you answered with "b," the more likely you are to love with your heart. This is clearly not a definitive test, just a tool to get you reflecting on your style. More often than not, the husband is more analytical and the wife is more sympathetic, but not always. The point is that empathy requires both the capacity to feel with another person and the objective capacity to step back and see how accurately those feelings match our partner's. Take another stab at assessing where you are by marking the following scale:

Thinking   Feeling

1   2   3   4   5   6   7   8   9   10

To improve your empathy skills, think of a specific recent situation that involved a misunderstanding—big or small—with your spouse. As you recount this experience, try to see it from her point of view. Why do you think she may have reacted or felt the way she did at that moment? Make a quick note of what you think was going on for her.

____

____

____

____

____

____

Now, ask your wife to rate how accurate your perceptions are on a scale of 1 to 10. Do this simple exercise as many times as you can in the next week or so. The more you do it, the more accurate you will become, and the more empathy you will have for each other.

Exercise 20:

ASSESSING YOUR SPIRITUAL LANGUAGE

Understanding what spiritual language you tend to speak most often can be enlightening, to say the very least, for most of us. And when you understand the spiritual language your spouse speaks, it can be revolutionary. After reviewing the nine differing pathways to God that are outlined in the book, rank the top two or three styles that fit you, and then your spouse, best.

Me   My wife   *The Pathway of . . .*

_____   _____   *Tradition:* loving God through rituals, sacraments, and symbols.

_____   _____   *Vision:* loving God by dreaming a great dream.

_____   _____   *Relationships:* loving God by being around other people.

_____   _____   *Intellectual Thought:* seeking God with the mind.

_____   _____   *Service:* loving God by loving others.

_____   _____   *Contemplation:* loving God in a quiet pursuit.

_____   _____   *Activism:* loving God by warring against injustice.

_____   _____   *Nature:* feeling closest to God in the out of doors.

_____   _____   *Worship:* loving God through joyful celebration.

Now, jot down some specific ways these are manifested in your life. If you are a Contemplative, for example, what do you like to do, where do you like to go, how much time do you like to spend, to be close to God?

____

____

____

____

____

____

Once you and your spouse have both noted the top two or three styles that fit you best, spend a few minutes comparing them. Discuss what you might learn from each other's pathways if they are different.

Exercise 21:

FINDING THE INSPIRATION AROUND YOU

The cultivation of inspiration is one of the most defining qualities of couples who have learned to become soul mates. As you walk together with God, few things will join your spirits like a moment that inspires both of you. This exercise will help you recount these moments and find new ones.

What happens within you, personally, when you are inspired by something you've read, heard, or seen? Do you have a physiological response? Are you more motivated? What about your emotions? Consider these questions and begin this exercise by completing this sentence: *I know I've been inspired when . . .*

____

____

____

____

Next, note the last time you were truly inspired (How long ago was it? What inspired you? Did you share it with anyone?):

____

____

____

____

Note two or three of the most inspirational moments of your entire life and why they stand out to you (consider speeches or sermons you've heard, books you've read, movies you've seen, people you've met, and so on):

____

____

____

____

Now consider how you can bring more inspirational moments into your marriage by answering the following questions together as a couple:

1. What kinds of places are we most likely to encounter inspirational moments (e.g., a site with historical significance, our church, hiking in the wilderness)?

2. Where are we as a couple likely to encounter people that might inspire us (e.g., a volunteer agency, a children's center)?

3. What things can we do together that would heighten our inspiration quotient (e.g., rent movies of motivational stories, read a biography of a couple that overcame something that seemed insurmountable)?

4. What couples can we socialize with or even ask to mentor us that would likely bring more inspirational moments into our marriage (e.g., an older couple at church that has a story to tell)?

Inspirational moments cannot be coerced or conjured up at will. They are discovered. Spontaneously. But we can avail our spirits of the places, the people, and the experiences where they are more likely to occur. As you review your answers to the previous questions together, make a commitment to look for the inspiration around you. As you've learned from the book, if we keep our eyes open, we often find what we are looking for.

Meditations on Proverbs for Couples

Previously published as Like a Kiss on the Lips

Les & Leslie Parrott

Drs. Les & Leslie Parrott know that wisdom is the bedrock of a healthy marriage. Great marriages are great because they're continually being shaped by enduring principles set forth centuries ago by Israel's wisest king, Solomon. In *Meditations on Proverbs for Couples*, the Parrotts share refreshing, down-to-earth reflections, brought home by candid vignettes from their own marriage and other true-life examples.

Meditations on Proverbs for Couples imparts choice gems from the richest treasury of practical wisdom ever known—the book of Proverbs. A marriage built on wisdom is one where hearts are open, faith is shared, personal growth is encouraged, dreams are nurtured, individual strengths are appreciated, romance flourishes, and even fights lead to deeper care and understanding.

Filled with thought-provoking questions and meditations, *Meditations on Proverbs for Couples* is a great way to join hearts and minds while laying wisdom for the foundation of a strong, happy relationship.

Hardcover 0-310-23446-8

Pick up a copy today at your favorite bookstore!

ZONDERVAN™

GRAND RAPIDS, MICHIGAN 49530
WWW.ZONDERVAN.COM

Marriage Devotional Bible

For All Seasons of Marriage

YOU WANT YOUR MARRIAGE TO BE THE BEST IT CAN BE—

Strong in commitment
Caring in communication
Joyous in lovemaking
United in vision
Above all, you want it to be grounded in faith.

Whether you're celebrating your fifth or twenty-fifth anniversary, if you long for deep satisfying intimacy with God and with your mate, the *Marriage Devotional Bible* is for you.

MORE THAN EXPERT INSIGHT

Les and Leslie Parrott, David and Claudia Arp, and Robert and Rosemary Barnes offer more than professional knowledge. They've worked out in their own marriages the truths they share with you in the *Marriage Devotional Bible*.

- The 260 daily devotions by these three couples show firsthand how God's Word intersects with the realities and rewards of marriage.

- And 52 weekend devotions help you and your mate connect through the "Weekend Warmup" questions for discussion.

- Other features include "Couples in the Bible" (both good and bad), book introductions, and "Just Between You and Me" questionnaires.

- And—best of all—the *Marriage Devotional Bible* is in the best-selling New International Version.

KEEP YOUR MARRIAGE GOING STRONG

If you're ready for new growth and depth in your marriage, now is the time to make it happen. Use this Bible, and you'll discover that your future together can be even better than your past.

NIV Translation   Size 5 1/2 x 8 1/2"

Hardcover	ISBN 0-310-90133-2
Softcover	ISBN 0-310-90878-7
Burgundy Bonded Leather	ISBN 0-310-91120-6

Pick up a copy today at your favorite bookstore!

GRAND RAPIDS, MICHIGAN 49530

WWW.ZONDERVAN.COM